Acquiring Knowledge of Legalese

Acquiring Knowledge of Legalese

Table Of Contents

Foreword

Prior to beginning an at home business venture it would be wise to consider a few different issues first. It is extremely important that you look into these matters because most businesses that neglect to do so fail in the long run.

Learning The Legalese
A Guide To Legal Planning For Home Business

Chapter 1:

Synopsis

The following information might be thought of as somewhat basic but nonetheless it is still quite important.

The Basics

Trading laws – Having extensive knowledge about the legislation involved in trade would be very beneficial. This is especially true if the business plans on conducting trade of product or services with the general public.

When considering these legalities, everything needs to be included, from the description of the product, the quality of the product, any guarantees and any other description of the product. It is very important that any guarantees that are made are met accordingly. Neglecting to do so will surely spell out failure for your business and you will also likely face legal consequences.

Terms of trading – when there is a connection made based on the business makeup with the public and other business entities, there is a need to get the terms and conditions of the business procedures sorted out. This is very important and directly affects the trading arrangements. These usually cover elements such as the payment terms, the transfer of titles due to the successful sale, the estimates for work done, the title of goods, failure to perform up to the contract stipulations and any other contractual inclusions.

Employment of staff - should the business expansion require the employment of staff, here too there are some legal implications that should be explored. This is to ensure the individual is well covered under the law and also to ensure all labor law requirements are met.

Chapter 2:

Synopsis

This is a business style that requires the individual to be declared as a single entity with the business linked for the main purpose of tax and all liability purposes. The sole proprietorship is a company in which the registration is done with the governing body of the time, in a limited liability framework of the company or corporation frame.

Sole Proprietor

Commonly the owner of the said business entity does not have to pay any income tax separate from the company but does have to have proper records of income and losses shown.

This should be reflected in the income tax returns filed. Here the owner of the business entity is inseparable from the sole proprietorship and thus is liable for any business debts the said business may incur through the course of the business lifespan.

Most new home based business entities chose this form of legal registration for its minimal requirements and legal obligations.

The main point to understand is that the owner of the business is liable in all ways to any debts incurred thus it helps to ensure the careful consideration on the part of the owner whenever he or she conducts any business.

The sole proprietor may use a trade name or business name which has no bearing at all on the owner's name. However there are some places that require the legal name of the owner to be clearly stated for the records.

Although the advantages do sometimes outweigh the disadvantages there is still a need to be sure that this is the most suitable option for the intended business endeavor.

The ability to raise capital is also not limited to any platform and can be done publicly or privately through investors. This ideally limits the risks of the office bearers if any and also the investors.

However for some this is not a good option as they really have very little say in how the money is going to be utilized for the business.

Chapter 3:

Synopsis

LLC is commonly used as an abbreviation for the term used for the limited liability company or a shorter version which is just limited company. Here the various elements of partnership and corporate structure are well blended to form the business transactions and liability issues.

LLC

This is a rather popular form for the business registration as it ideally creates, as its name depicts limited liability issues. The flexibility of this enterprise blends the best of both the partnership and corporate elements to form a desirable legal platform.

The organizational structure does not need to be designed around the projected profits thus making it an ideal form of business structure.

This in fact contributes to the taxation procedures that are quite adoptable and beneficial to certain parties. The business entity is based on the unincorporated association and not just the corporation platform which would constitute the primary element of the limited liability and characteristic of the partnership in which the income taxation does not apply.

The charging order mechanism creates the protection for the membership interest and the partnership interests at a significant level. This system limits the creditors to a particular debt member or partner without conferring any voting or managing rights on the creditor.

There is also the presence of the flexibility and default rules which are quite in favor of the members within the LLC.

Set in place to create the flexibility on how to govern the respective LLCs it proves time and again to be a viable option for many. It is also conducive, as it can be implemented whichever way deemed fit as long as it stays within the legal boundaries set.

Other advantages would include having the options to choose the taxation platform best suited and exploited for the purpose of keeping the outgoing payment to the minimal.

Chapter 4:

Incorporating

Synopsis

This particular business acknowledgement is done in the form of creating a new corporation which is a legal entity is recognizable as an individual under the law. This recognition will deem the entity fit to be looked upon as a business, a nonprofit organization, sports entity, or a governing body overseeing a particular are. This may be listed as a city, town or a collective designated area.

Incorporation

One of the more dominant benefits of this style of business registration in the limiting of the liabilities of those listed within the company.

This would ultimately mean that personal assets of those involved in the business entity will not used to pay of creditor claims and lawsuits.

The guaranteed protection on the personal assets is part of the stipulations within this particular business option. The only commitment the individual involved are like to lose should the business not be a successful as anticipated is the initial invested amount.

This arrangement applies even if one party of the members in involved in a lawsuit of sort, thus ensuring the legally the creditors cannot infringe upon the business entity as a whole to collect on the afore mentioned party's debt.

In terms of transferable ownership stipulations it is rather friendly in nature and in some areas documentation is not even needed or insisted upon.

This would mean that there would be no legal requirement to file or record such changes in the original ownership. This form of business registration can usually continue indefinitely even when there are deaths within the original group members.

It should also be noted in the naming of the business entity under the incorporate style there should be three distinctive element clearly displayed.

This would include the first being the distinctive, the second being the descriptive and the third being the definition of the type of legal platform chosen.

Chapter 5:

Tax Planning

Synopsis

More often than not people tend to dread the tax filing process, thus leaving it to the very last possible minute to get it done. However with a little planning this tax planning process can yield surprisingly good results. Taking time to prepare for this tax filing exercise right through the year helps to make the task easier and more systematic.

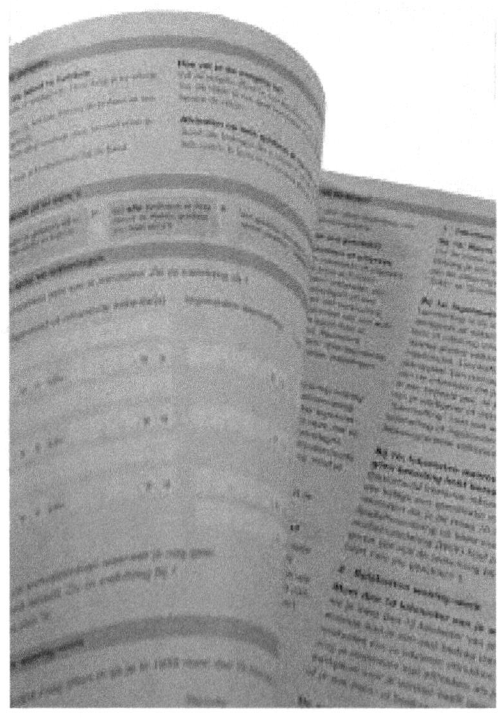

Taxes

The following are some areas that should be considered when trying to implement effective tax planning exercises:

Generally every individual is expected to keep good records and books on the outgoing and incoming funds through a suitable accounting system.

This is not hard to do if the exercise is done in a disciplined and systematic way. Keeping complete and accurate records will help to maximize the various applications for deductions made.

These deductions can be for travel, entertainment, expenses and any others spending that would be utilized during the course of the business venture over a specific period of time.

Backing all these notifications with the supporting receipts and other documentations is also equally important. Claims made without relevant supporting documentation will not be entertained.

There is also the need to understand the home office deduction rules and how it applied to the individual claims and business accounts.

Knowing what to write off legally will ensure the best possible tax reliefs are given. Tax claims can also be made on transport mileage but this also has to be supported with the relevant receipts.

Records have to be kept on each trip's mileage, the date, the purpose of the trip and its destination.

If all these step are taken and some semblance of records are kept then there should be less need to pay high fees to get professional help when it comes to filing tax returns.

With the bulk of the work already done throughout the year, everything else that is left to do would be quite easy in comparison and certainly cheaper.

Chapter 6:
Financial Planning

Synopsis

The financial planning that should be considered before even embarking on the home business is something that most people are wise enough to look into. However the extent of the knowledge applied leaves much to be desired and often the home business owner is faced with unpleasant surprises due to the inadequate knowledge and planning of the financial aspect of the business.

Finances

The following are some of the areas that should be given utmost attention:

Ensuring that there is a separate account for the business itself is something that should not be compromised upon. Setting up such an account will ensure all business transactions are clearly recorded and visible at a moment's notice.

This is a comparatively better option that having the additional workload of separating unrelated matters when a common account is used.

Consulting an accountant is also another advantage the home business owner should consider. Sometimes it is better and easier to engage the expertise of those who know what they are doing rather than create a stressful situation that would eventually affect other aspect of the business.

These accountants especially the ones who specialize in taxation laws and accounts, would be able to advise the individual on any additional tax breaks that may not already have been used.

Insurance is also another issue to consider when working through the financial planning stage. Getting coverage for equipment and possible employees will have to be considered. Insuring the inventory may also be considered as this would cause considerable loses should any unfortunate incident occur.

Being aware of any state laws that would have a bearing on the financials of any home business is also important to explore. This is to ensure there are no legal ramifications somewhere down the line of the business venture. All the relevant licenses should also be acquired and factored into the financial planning exercise.

Chapter 7:

Business Partners

Synopsis

Although most businesses start out as individual commitments sometimes this commitment may prove to be so overwhelming that there is a need to bring in outside help in the form of business partners. If this is the option chosen by the individual there should be some points explored and understood before embarking on a suitable partnership drive.

Partners

With the addition of a partnership there is the opportunity to pool the capital and management resources to grow the business further or to help run the already successfully expanding scenario.

There are two very basic types of partnerships and that would the limited partnership and the general partnership. The general partnership is relatively easy to establish as it only requires the names to be included and an agreement to be drawn up stating the various rights and responsibilities of each party within the business partnership platform.

The advantages of the general partnership would include the simplicity of the organization basics, the additional personal resources either financial or managerial in its capacity, the low start up cost, limited outside regulations and no possibility of double taxation.

As for the limited partnership the points vary a little whereby the investor liability is limited to the amount agreed upon as the investment capital share of the partner.

In most cases the limited partnership function is only that of providing additional funds for the business without having any say in the daily running of the said business entity.

The advantages of this type of partnership would include the retaining of complete control by the original general partner and the limited investment would equal limited liability incurred if any.

It's also an easy way to secure additional capital without the hassle of extensive documentation and there are no direct taxation conforming requirements.

Therefore with these options to choose from the individual has to decide which one is best for the business expansion and for the individual personal preference.

Chapter 8:

Using Online Legal Services And Documents

Synopsis

As with any endeavor there is bound to be some sort of documentation requirement involved, therefore it is important to have some knowledge of what kinds of documents are needed for the home business set up in order to ensure it is legal. Besides documentation there is also the legal considerations that should be looked into as this too will have some bearing of the future of the business.

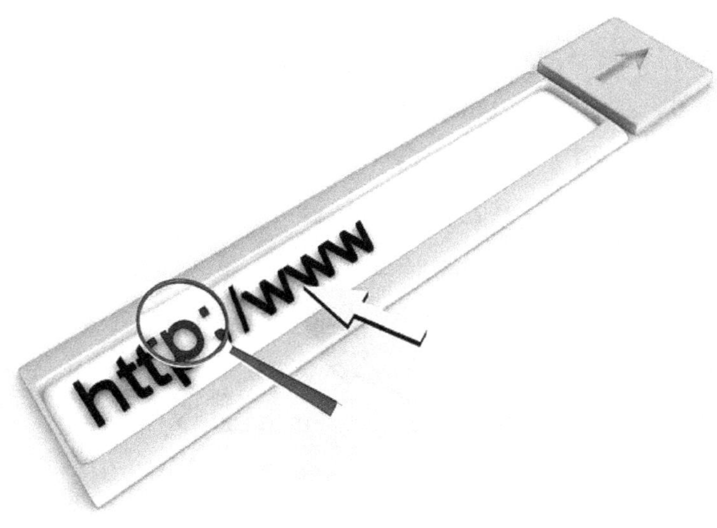

The Net

Some of the documentations may include agreements, if there is more than one individual involved in the new home business, contractor forms, corporation forms, credit forms, employments forms if there is any intention of eventually acquiring a team of staff to work on the business, entertainment form for the purpose of keeping track of such expenses for tax filings, power of attorney should any future problem arise such as a death and many others.

For the individual starting out on the home business there are also other forms to consider such as buy and sell agreements, copyrights, contract of deed, patents, promissory notes and trademarks are just some of the more common ones used.

When it come to addressing the legal side of the home businesses needs there are also other guides that should be used such as attaining legal preparation services, considering lawyer recommendations, attaining information on specific state and governing laws that may have some impact to the business and for some businesses that are guideline books available for perusal to ensure no unpleasant surprises come up midway through the business which would jeopardize the entire business's future.

There are also other documents available for use within the actual business functioning part, which the home business owner may want to consider in order to help provide some form of virtual assistance especially if the business style consists of only one individual.

Chapter 9:

Why It's Dangerous To Not Have The Legalities In Order

Synopsis

The following are some of the points to consider in the quest to ensure all legalities are adhered to:

Important Points

Deciding on the form the business is to take on is perhaps one of the more important issues to tackle as this will set the frame work for the business style and processes. The easiest and most commonly used would be that of the sole proprietorship for its more obvious benefits.

There is also the registration of the business name to consider. This requirement should be followed if the name to be used for the business differs from that of the owner's. This legality is important to assure the public that the business entity is identifiable and legitimate. A general search is usually done by the relevant parties to ensure the name chosen for the business is not already in use.

Acquiring the proper and befitting license for the particular business style is also another factor to consider as anything unlicensed is usually considered illegal under any law. However it should be noted here that the licensing procedures may vary depending on the state and the governing body at the time.

The responsibility of filling income tax lies on the owner of the business and this should be done is a systematic and honest way. Avoiding any scrutiny by the relevant legal parties would be a good idea; as such complications can only bring further problems which might adversely affect the business.

Wrapping Up

Being aware of the various legal implications when considering a home based business endeavor is very important to ensuring there are no complications and problems during the course of the business history. Avoiding such negative circumstances through the proper legalized daily functioning aspects of the business should be a priority set in place at the very beginning.